Marion T. Lane

Where Did We Come From: The Birth of Black America?

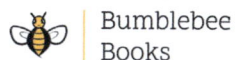
Bumblebee Books

BUMBLEBEE PAPERBACK EDITION
Copyright © Marion T. Lane 2023

The right of Marion T. Lane to be identified as author of
this work has been asserted in accordance with sections 77 and 78
of the Copyright, Designs and Patents Act 1988.

All Rights Reserved

No reproduction, copy or transmission of this publication
may be made without written permission.
No paragraph of this publication may be reproduced,
copied or transmitted save with the written permission of the publisher,
or in accordance with the provisions
of the Copyright Act 1956 (as amended).

Any person who commits any unauthorised act in relation
to this publication may be liable to criminal
prosecution and civil claims for damage.

A CIP catalogue record for this title is
available from the British Library.

ISBN: 978-1-83934-313-1
Bumblebee Books is an imprint of
Olympia Publishers.

First Published in 2023

Bumblebee Books
Tallis House
2 Tallis Street
London
EC4Y 0AB

Printed in Great Britain

Dedication

This story is dedicated to my ancestors

Where Did We Come from: The Birth of Black America

Table of Contents

Chapter 1: The World Stage

Chapter 2: How Did Africans Arrive?

Chapter 3: How Were They Treated?

Chapter 4: The Great Change

Chapter 5: Slavery

Chapter 1
The World Stage

Jeremy and his great grandfather were watching television when Pop-pop mentioned they would be getting new next door neighbors. The family is supposed to move in within two weeks. They are from Venezuela a country in South America.

Jeremy asked his great grandfather, "Where did we come from? I mean where did African Americans come from?"

Pop-pop began to explain that thirteen years before the Pilgrims landed at Plymouth, Massachusetts on the Mayflower, 104 English settlers arrived at Jamestowne Island in Virginia on May 14, 1607. Jamestowne was the first successful British colonial settlement.

Many of the original colonists were rich people who brought their indentured servants with them. Although the British were the first to establish a permanent English colony, Holland, Sweden, France and Spain also established colonies.

Indentured servants were generally poor people who worked for someone, under a contract, for up to seven years and then they were free to do what they wanted. Many times they were given land as payment for their services and they became farmers. Sometimes they purchased land with their earnings. The colonists did not like hard labor and had a difficult time getting along with the Indians. Therefore, some of them returned to Europe.

During this same time, Portugal was a world trading power. They traded in spices, precious metals, cloth and slaves. The Portuguese had been trading with the people of the Kingdom of Angola in Africa for many years.

The people of the Kingdom of Angola were highly skilled craftsmen. They were expert farmers, carpenters, cloth makers, basket makers, metal workers and artisans. Their country was rich with gold and silver.

The Angolans had been trading their products with several countries for a long time.

Jeremy was very surprised to learn about Angola. He asked Pop-pop if they were wealthy because of their trading. Pop-pop said that they lived a comfortable life because of it.

He also explained to Jeremy that Christianity had been introduced to them in 1491 by the Portuguese.

Chapter 2
How Did the Africans Arrive?

During this period of time, Portugal and Spain were joined in an agreement called the Iberian Union. This agreement included all of their ships flying two flags, the flag of Spain and the flag of Portugal.

Also, both countries had several territories in other parts of the world. They were running ships between their territories selling goods.

Even though Portugal had been trading with the people of Angola for many years, they decided to make it one of their territories. Therefore, in 1618 Portugal invaded Angola.

Jeremy asked, "To take it over?"

Pop-pop answered, "Yes, to take it over."

However, the people resisted. They could not understand the takeover since they had been trading with Portugal for so long.

During the takeover, around 50,000 Angolans were captured for resisting and held as captives. In a short period of time, the Portuguese found that it was too costly to feed the captives and too costly to guard them.

Jeremy asked, "Did they let them go?"

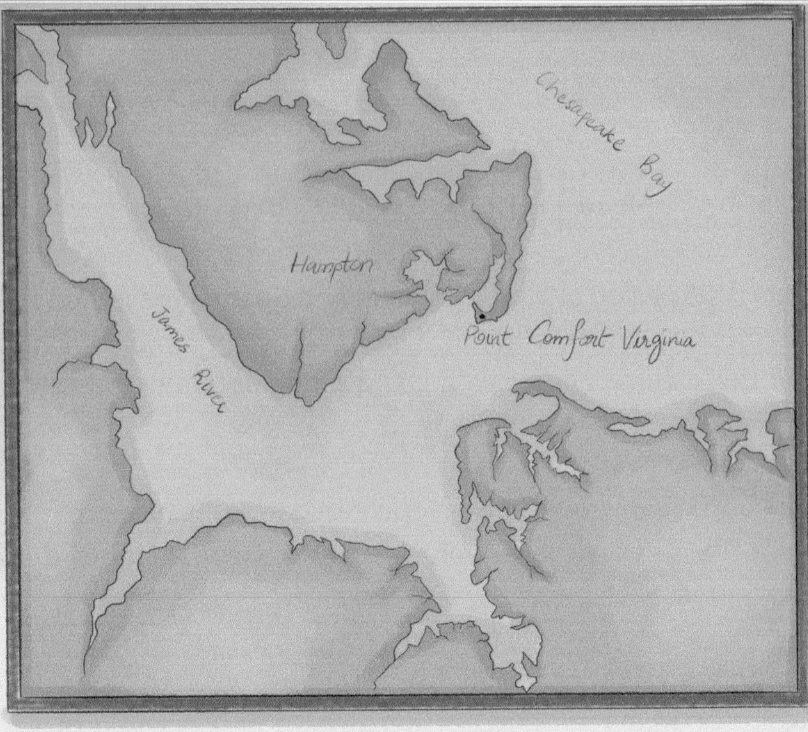
Chesapeake Bay
Hampton
James River
Point Comfort Virginia

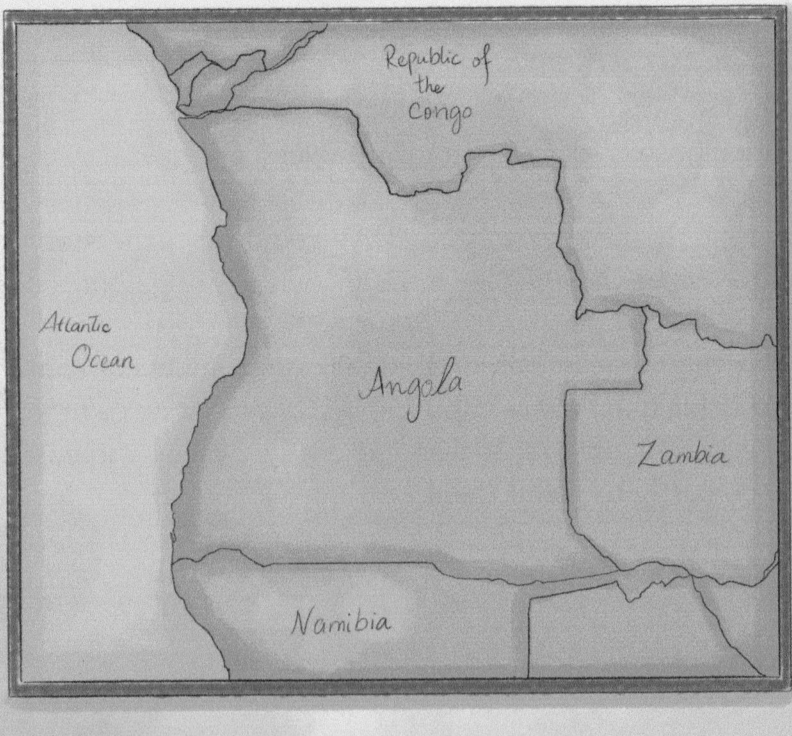
Republic of the Congo
Atlantic Ocean
Angola
Zambia
Namibia

Pop-pop replied they did not let them go. The Portuguese decided to ship them to other places around the world and sell them into slavery. "Oh no!" said Jeremy.

Next, they placed 350 of these captives on board a very large galleon or ship called the San Juan Bautista. The San Juan Bautista was then sent on its way to Veracruz, Mexico to sell them as slaves.

Now, the people of the Netherlands were trying to get their independence from Spain. Since the Netherlands was a very small country, they had a creative way to fight for their independence.

"What did they do?" Jeremy asked.

They would hire privateers to fight for them. The privateers were ships under contract, a Marquee, who would sail under the Dutch flag, the flag of the Netherlands. These ships were instructed to look for any ship flying a Spanish flag, engage it with gunfire, board the ship and take off the bounty or goods. The privateer would get to keep the bounty to sell.

"Wow!" said Jeremy.

Two British privateers, the White Lion and the Treasurer, flying a Dutch flag, spotted the San Juan Bautista flying the flags of Spain and Portugal and approached it. The White Lion exchanged gunfire and the men went on board. They were looking for silver and/or gold but only found the 350 captives. Therefore, they were very disappointed.

The men of the White Lion and the Treasurer decided to take off 60 of the captives. Knowing the people in Jamestowne needed workers, they headed towards Jamestowne with the captives.

The first documented Africans arrived on the White Lion in Virginia in 1619. They arrived at Point Comfort, now Hampton, Virginia, in August of 1619. The Treasure took the rest of the captives to Bermuda.

Chapter 3

How Were They Treated?

Following their arrival, Pocahontas' husband, John Rolfe, wrote that some 20 and odd Africans arrived in August of 1619. Actually, 32 of the 60 Angolans were left: 15 males and 17 females. John Rolfe wrote "some 20 and odd" because they were men women and children. The rest of the Angolans were taken on to Bermuda.

Originally, the Angolans were not enslaved. Pop-pop stated that the first Africans were treated as servants when they arrived.

Jeremy asked Pop-pop why were they treated as servants.

Pop-pop clarified that they were Christian and at the time the British did not enslave Christians.

Jeremy asked, "Were there other Christians in Africa?"

"Yes!" responded Pop-pop.

A good example of another Christian country was the Kingdom of the Kongo. This country shared a border with the Kingdom of Angola. Afonso I ruled this kingdom from 1508 to 1542. He changed or converted 80% of the people to Christianity.

An important fact to keep in mind is that British society was based on class and not race. In other words, people were divided based on if they were gentlemen, land owners, skilled workers and non- skilled workers.

The African indentured servants and British indentured servants socialized together and married. They also intermarried with the Native Americans. Intermarriage was not stopped by law in Virginia until 1691.

Chapter 4

The Great Change

As time passed, more and more of the 50,000 captured Angolans arrived in the various colonies and so did European indentured servants. The practice of indentured servitude continued for many years. At the end of their contracts, the servants received "freedom dues." They received payment in cash or land as payment. Most of them purchased land with the cash they received.

Jeremy asked his great-grandfather when did things begin to change. Pop-pop told Jeremy because the indentured servants received "freedom dues." At the end of their contracts for their service, this practice became very costly for the wealthy land owners.

Therefore, the wealthy land owners began to extend the length of the contracts. The time of the contracts increased from 4 to 7 years; to 10 years; then until a person turned 21 years of age; and finally until a person turned 28 years of age.

The initial purpose for the contract or indenture was to work off the cost of the person's transportation to North America. However, the landowners found over time the free labor helped to increase their wealth.

By 1641, the practice of owning Africans as slaves for life came to be. Slavery was first established by law in Massachusetts around this time.

"How was slavery different?" Jeremy asked.

His great-grandfather explained that slavery was a life-long condition that could pass from parent to child. Slavery took away contracts and "freedom dues." The people had to work without the idea of owning land and becoming free.

Jeremy stated that "slavery" did not seem very fair to him.

Many more people began to arrive in North America from other countries in Africa and the Virgin Islands. In Virginia, some of the people arriving were not able to hold onto their status as indentured servants. For example, John Punch a runaway indentured servant, became the first slave for life in Virginia in 1640. Some arriving were not Christian and, therefore, were enslaved.

In 1667, Baptism as a Christian no longer granted freedom. It was also decided that children would share the status of the mother. For example, if the mother was an indentured servant the child would be indentured. If the mother was enslaved, then the child would be enslaved.

As each of the various 13 colonies developed, they operated as separate countries. Therefore, slavery was not fully activated by law in Virginia until 1705.

Chapter 5

Slavery

Jeremy wanted to know if African people could own slaves. Pop-pop told him they could and some did own slaves. They tended to purchase family members. However, they were not permitted to own European indentured servants after 1667.

"What was slavery like?" asked Jeremy.

Pop-pop explained, life was very difficult for enslaved people. Slaves could not gather in large numbers; they could not have guns or ammunition; they could not leave the plantation without written permission; they could not have jury trials; and they worked from sun rise to sunset.

Some slave owners were compassionate, however, many were not. A slave owner was permitted to use whatever punishment he wanted on an enslaved person. The owner would not get into trouble for what harm he inflicted. Also, families were separated by being sold.

A major slight was the fact that enslaved people were not permitted to learn to read or write.

"Why?" asked Jeremy.

He could not imagine why they were not allowed to read or write.

Many historians have different opinions as to why this was the practice. However, if a person could not read or write, they could not learn the laws or the court system. They would have a difficult time transacting business to buy their freedom. Not having these skills limits a persons' ability improve their status. The same as it does today.

For example, there was an important court case in England called the Somerset Decision. In 1772, the judge, Lord Mansfield, ruled that British "statutory" law nor British "common" law supported slavery.

Just imagine, if enslaved people could read or write, they would have learned about this case and would have been able to stop their mistreatment. The laws of the colonies were based on British law.

Jeremy stated, "I am glad that I can read and write."

Pop-pop went on to say that being able to read and write is protection from mistreatment and insures freedom, "Always remember that fact."

Sources Consulted

Hashaw, Tim. *The Birth of Black America: The First African Americans and the Pursuit of Freedom at Jamestown.* Carroll & Graf Publishers, 2007.

Hashaw, Tim. *Children of Perdition.* Mercer, 2007.

Price, David A. *Love and Hate in Jamestown.* Knoff Publishers, 2003

About the Author

Marion T. Lane, Ed.D. is one of the few African American members of the National Society of the Daughters of the American Revolution, the National Gavel Society, the National Society of Colonial Daughters of the 17th Century, the National Society of Colonial Dames of the XVII Century, the Jamestowne Society and served as the National President of the Society of Descendants of Washington's Army at Valley Forge (2010-2014). In addition, this retired educator (38 years) serves on the Board of the Museum of the American Revolution.